BLACK AMERICA FACES ECONOMIC CRISIS
SOLUTIONS MADE SIMPLE

Dr. Rosie Milligan

BLACK AMERICA FACES ECONOMIC CRISIS
SOLUTIONS MADE SIMPLE

YOU WILL LEARN:

- What Every Black Person—Professional, Celebrity, And Otherwise—Must Do.
- The Role Of The Black Church.
- Why Education For Blacks Must Be Relevant To Their Success In A Racist Society.

AND MUCH MORE!

Dr. Rosie Milligan

MILLIGAN BOOKS, INC. **BOOKS** CALIFORNIA

Copyright © 2008 by Dr. Rosie Milligan
Los Angeles, California
All Rights Reserved

Printed and Bound in the United States of America
Published and Distributed by:
Milligan Books

Book design by Milligan Books
Cover layout by Kevin Allen

First Printing,
10 9 8 7 6 5 4 3 2 1

ISBN 978-0-9815783-0-9

Library of Congress Cataloging-in-Publication Data
Milligan, Rosie Dr.
Black America Faces Economic Crisis: Solutions Made Simple, Dr. Rosie
Milligan

1. Social Studies 2. Self-Help

Milligan Books, Inc.
1425 W. Manchester Ave., Suite C
Los Angeles, California 90047
www.milliganbooks.com
drrosie@aol.com
(323) 750-3592

Dedication

This book is dedicated to all who made great sacrifice that the next generation may have a better economic life.

This book is also dedicated to Muhammad Nassardeen, founder of Recycling Black Dollars, a business legend, and an icon that embodied all that he preached—"Put a dollar in the Black man's hand every time you have a chance!" "Mo," this book is from both of us because as I write, I can yet hear your voice; see your brilliant smile; and feel your spirit. Man, I miss you!

Farewell and Well Done
Muhammad Nassardeen

by Dr. Rosie Milligan

The African-American community revisits a moment that's too familiar—the demise of a great leader—Muhammad Nassardeen. Muhammad was the founder of the organization *Recycling Black Dollars*. He was a visionary and a business guru. His concern for the dismal economic plight of the African-American family and community led him to leave a six-figure income corporate job to try and change the economic direction of Black folk.

Nassardeen, in my opinion, understood what fuels the engine that turns the economic key. Daily, many Black leaders, preachers, and politicians spit rhetoric about how many times the dollar bounces in the Black community versus how many times it bounces for other races. Nassardeen understood that entrepreneurship was the bases for economic empowerment. He recognized that Black business ownership would yield more jobs for Blacks, and that if Blacks did not own the businesses in their communities, where Black people spend a majority of their spendable income, then the Black dollars would continue to leave the Black community. Being cognitive of those facts, he was driven to focus on changing the attitude of Blacks about business ownership and supporting Black businesses.

I will mention a few of the tasks Muhammad spearheaded, although to adequately cover all of this great man's accomplishments, I would need to write a whole book. His works encompass picking up the baton from Marcus Garvey, W.E.B. Dubois, Dr. Martin Luther King Jr., and Malcolm X. He possessed all their spirits—he loved Black people. He was not one with diarrhea of the mouth and paralysis of the hands and feet; nor was he a man with faith and no works. He was about what he believed in—and he believed that Blacks could do for themselves.

When Black-owned gas stations were struggling, Nassardeen brought the issue before the Black community. He kept the spotlight on the whereabouts of Black businessmen. For years he facilitated weekly meetings. He had each business owner to give a sixty-second commercial about their businesses and to tell what Black business they had supported that week, then how to "speak up" and "shut up." Each non-business owner would introduce themselves and tell what businesses they supported.

Muhammad puts the "B" in the words "Black business." He started the *Recycling Black Dollars Black Business Directory* so that Blacks could find Black-owned businesses. He led the *Change Bank Crusade*, which drove millions of dollars into Black banks (Founders and Broadway Federal). He was the catalyst behind the *Annual Business Competition*, which awarded $20,000 for the best business plan. He rented office space that was large enough to share with other entrepreneurs. He was never about the spotlight for himself; he wanted the spotlight focused on Black businesses and the needs of Blacks.

He recognized that the image depicted of Blacks in the media had caused many Blacks to see themselves from the lens of the media. The image we have of a person or race dictates the attitudes and behaviors that we hold towards them. He understood the impact of media and image. He wanted to right all wrongs and to fix every dilemma the Black man faced. He started his own newspaper to highlight the good things about Black folks. He hosted a radio talk show, *On the Positive Side*. He held an annual recognition luncheon, spotlighting Black achievements.

Muhammad was likened unto biblical characters, such as John the Baptist, who was crying, "Repent." Nassardeen cried out to Blacks to change their ways. He would tell us to "put a dollar in the Black man's hand every time you get a chance." He forced his legs to carry him in spite of the pain. He would not give in or give up. Like Jeremiah, he could not quit. Like David when everyone else was afraid of the giant, Goliath, David merely took what little he had and went for it. Nassardeen didn't have much, but he took what he had and went for it with all his might. Like Nehemiah, who could have been comfortable in the king's palace, his countenance was sad because his "homeland lieth in waste and the gates burned down." Nassardeen could have been comfortable with his six-figure income in corporate America. But instead, he, like Nehemiah, left a place of comfort to help rebuild the walls of the Black community that lieth in waste since the 1965 Riot and from the Rodney King Uprising. I still call it the Rodney King Riot.

What would Muhammad want us to do—cry, mourn, or give long, elegant speeches? The answer is none of these things! He would want us to continue to do for ourselves—starting businesses, supporting Black-owned businesses, putting our money in Black banks, and educating our children. He would want Black men to take care of their families and to "put a dollar in a Black hand whenever you can."

Muhammad Nassardeen—his story and his journey must be told! We talked about it last week. He would always say to me, "Doc, I know, and I'm going to finish my book. In fact, I will have it for your next Black Writers on Tour."

I am going to miss you, Nassardeen.

Acknowledgment

I want to thank the late Muhammad Nassardeen, founder of Recycle Black Dollars for always reminding Blacks to make supporting Black businesses a priority. I want to thank his family for allowing him to share his time and resource with so many people.

I want to thank my friend, the late Mary Crump, who believed in Black folk. She invested in many community entrepreneurs business ventures

To my children, Pamela Milligan-McGee, M.D., John Sherman Milligan, Jr. and Cedric Andre Milligan, I thank you for helping with all my multiple businesses. It is because of you that I have been able to spread my wings. You are the wind beneath my wings. May you train your children as I have trained you, to be self-determine.

To Mr. John Milligan, Sr., thank you for helping me with the new technology and for keeping my computers updated.

To my goddaughter, Rita Hall, I am so proud of your accomplishments, and the work that you do to help so many charitable causes. You remind me so much of me. I love you, Ms. Rita.

To my sisters, Clara Hunter King, ESQ, Kenyaka Beckley, Owen Lee Nelson, Margaret Hoskins and Willie Micou and to my brothers, Leroy Hunter and Robert Earl Hunter, I thank you for supporting my business.

To my business cheerleaders, L.C. Green, Thomas Sampson, Dr. Claud Anderson, Joe C. Hopkins, ESQ and Bishop Frank Stewart, Bishop L. J. Guillory—Ombudsman General, Dr. Maxine Thompson, Gayle Dickerson, my nephews—Minister Rufus Nelson and Minister Ricky Hoskins, and my son-in-law, Elder Kelvin McGee, all you have encouraged me to continue to believe that we will get to the finish line.

To all those who have helped me in any way, you know who you are and I want to thank you.

Dr. Rosie Milligan Biography

*Dr. Milligan's Motto: "Erase, No!—Step-Over, Can't!—
and Move Forward with Life!"*

D R. ROSIE MILLIGAN, REGISTERED NURSE, counselor/
health consultant, author, and Ph.D. in business admin-
istration, has always been an achiever. Every career or business
she's been involved in has included helping other people ac-
complish what they wanted in life. Her motto, "Erase, No!—
Step-Over, Can't!—and Move Forward with Life!" has been
a motivating influence for hundreds to whom she has been
mentor and role model.

The mother of three entrepreneurs—an M.D., a cosmetolo-
gist, and a health food store owner—Dr. Milligan lectures na-
tionally on economic empowerment, managing diversity in the
workplace, and male/female relationships. Her books, *Starting
a Business Made Simple, Getting Out of Debt Made Simple* and
Creating a New You in Six Weeks Made Simple, have helped
many across the country. Her most recent release, *Black Amer-*

ica Faces Economic Crisis: Solutions Made Simple, is a must-read. Dr. Milligan is also the author of thirteen other books.

Dr. Milligan has been an instructor in nursing education and was director of nursing for the College of Allied Health Careers and for the Los Angeles Job Corp Center. She assisted in writing the competency-based educational curriculum for Geriatric Nursing for the National Job Corp, was a former employee of United Health Plan (HMO) as nursing supervisor and staff development and holds lifetime teaching credentials with the state of California.

As an entrepreneur and economic empowerment activist, the Mississippi native co-owns a bookstore with her son. She owns Professional Business Consulting Services—providing consultation for new and small businesses and staff development training for corporations. In 1990, she started a publishing company, Milligan Books, where she has published over 150 new African-American authors in the past ten years. Her publishing company is the largest and fastest growing publishing company owned by an African-American female in the nation.

A successful motivational speaker and trainer, she has appeared on numerous television and radio shows, such as *Sally Jesse Raphael* in New York; *A.M. Philadelphia; Evening Exchange* in Washington, D.C., *Marilyn Kagan Show* in Los Angeles, *The Rob Nelson Show* in Los Angeles, and she's a regular guest on Stevie Wonder's KJLH Radio. She is founder and director of **"Black Writers on Tour,"** and a former columnist for *Black Issue Book Review Magazine.* Dr. Milligan Host her own Cable TV show—*Express Yourself Literary Café.* She is the publisher of the *Los Angeles Truth Newspaper*. Her articles have been published in major newspapers nationwide.

Dr. Milligan was recipient of the 1996 Pioneer Women Award—Los Angeles City Commission on the Status of Women and was also the recipient of the 2001 Ervin Magic Johnson Master of Money Award. Dr. Milligan was nominated for Best Community Leader in the Steve Harvey's 2004 Hoodie Awards. She was a former chairperson of the Community Advisory Group 8th District and former member of HOPE Toast Masters Chapter 1013 Los Angeles.

Dr. Milligan is obviously a woman who knows no limits and has proven this with her newest venture, Milligan Literary Agency. She has sold her work to some of the largest and most prestigious publishing houses.

Black America Faces Economic Crisis: Workable Solutions Made Simple, is a must-read. Dr. Milligan is also the author of ten other books.

Table of Contents

I HAD A DREAM ABOUT AFRICAN-AMERICANS

IN 1992, I HAD A dream about African-Americans. This dream inspired me to write the book, Negroes, Colored People, Blacks, and African Americans in America. In my dream, I saw the bones of African Americans scattered in a valley called "The Valley of the Dry Bones." In the dream, I was the only person alive. I was so afraid. I lifted my hands up in the air and cried, "Father, can these bones live?" A voice answered, "Yes, if you can connect the parts together the way they were." I found all the bones of the lower extremities, from the toes to the hip bones, except the ankle bones. I found all the bones from the hip bones to the head bones, but the chest bones were missing. I found bones from the shoulders to the fingers, but the wrist bones were missing. Flesh covered the body parts as they were discovered. I tried but was unable to stand the body erect because the ankle bones were missing. I could not put the heart in place because the chest bones were missing. I could not put the hands on because the wrist bones were missing.

I left the scene to search for help, hoping, by chance, that there might be someone else in the valley. I met a car driving backward down a steep hill. The driver had no flesh on his bones. I asked why he was driving backward and he said he was trying to see where he had been so that he could get a grip on where he could go again. I immediately woke up and heard a voice say, "Write what you saw—the problem and the solution."

I interpreted my dream thusly: The inability to stand the body erect represents succumbing to the images depicted by the Eurocentric media. The inability to place the heart represents loss of love, care, and support for Black businesses. The inability to attach the hands represents the lack of self-determination.

Introduction

USINESS OWNERSHIP AND MULTIPLE STREAMS of income are the only hope for saving Black America. Daily, many Black leaders, preachers, and politicians spit rhetoric about how many times the dollar bounces in the Black community versus how many times it bounces for other races. When we discuss the times a Black dollar bounces in the Black community in a negative way, we must understand that Black business ownership yields more jobs for blacks. If Blacks do not own the businesses in their communities, where they spend a majority of their spendable income, then Black dollars will continue to leave the Black community. Being cognizant

of these facts, we must focus on changing the attitude of Blacks about business ownership and supporting Black businesses.

Thirty-five years ago, I began preaching to Black folk about the importance of business ownership and multiple streams of income. I knew then that entre-preneurialship was the basis for economic empowerment.

It was very clear to me that jobs come from business—and that all races employ their own race first—and all other races hire Blacks last. Blacks were then—and continue to be—the last hired and the first fired. They are also the first to suffer from downsizing.

While many Black politicians were shouting, "Blacks need jobs," I was shouting, "Blacks need to own businesses—jobs do not perpetuate jobs for your children and other Blacks, but businesses do." It is important for Blacks to start their own businesses, and it is equally important for Blacks to support Black-owned businesses. Blacks must follow the business principle of "find a need and fill it." Even Black business owners must have multiple streams of income. New technology, new kinds of services, and new products can create new needs that can make your products or services obsolete. If you have income from other sources, you will have the opportunity to regroup.

Many Black-owned businesses are not passed down generationally, the reason being that most Black businesses are struggling versus flourishing. Our children need incentive or motivation to want to inherit a struggling business. They do not want to start their own business because they see too many businesses struggling, and have seen too many businesses fail.

Blacks starting their own businesses and Blacks supporting Black-owned businesses are the only hope we have for survival. Our schools—our educational systems—will have failed to do their job if they do not make entrepreneurialship a vocational option with as much emphasis placed on business ownership as is placed on getting an education in preparation for a job—and that's real!

I contend that it is the responsibility of every parent, childcare provider, legal guardian, school, politician, and Black preacher to encourage business ownership and to keep it in the forefront at all times. Every Black church should have a business directory, and the pastor should—from his mouth—encourage his members to support the business owners in his congregation and to seek out Black-owned business services in general.

After all, they should be aware of the fact that Blacks are in an economic crisis and that our survival is dependent upon Blacks doing for self. People

are coming to the United States to find a safe haven and to get a piece of the American pie for "them" and "theirs" and not for "us" and "ours." If others help us, that should be the gravy; however, we must bring our own meat to the table.

Marcus Garvey, W.E.B. Dubois, Elijah Muhammad, Malcolm X, Muhammad Nassardeen (of Recycling Black Dollars), Attorney Joe Hopkins, James Clingman, Dr. Claud Anderson, and the Honorable Minister Louis Farrakhan told us that we must do for self. When will we listen, and who will we obey?

What will it mean in the future to have a college education and yet, have to work on a job that does not require a college education, or to even be unemployed? I beg of you to take Black business ownership seriously. If you are happily working a job and are pleased with your salary, I admonish you to consider other streams of income, because jobs are just too unstable and unpredictable today

The following three paragraphs are excerpts from the book *The Monopoly System* written by William B. Thompson and Vincent P. Harris.

The salary from your job should be what sustains you until you find better and more efficient ways of creating money. Your salary from your job is not just for paying your bills; it is to be used to make investments that

will replace your salary. Your salary should become less important. Because of the assets you have purchased with your salary, you should have created enough cash flow to render your salary as unnecessary or less important—this is called playing the real life game of Monopoly.

If you are as dependant on your salary as you were when you started working ten years ago, your future will be one of regret and sorrow. If you continue this path, your retirement will be less than one-third of what you are earning. If you are struggling now with your full salary, what will your retirement status look like?

"If you lost your job, which you have made your only and permanent source of income, how do you maintain your lifestyle, pay your mortgage, make your car payments, and provide the necessities of life for your family?"

Think! Let's make the business of business ownership every Black person's business!

Nobody Knows The Trouble I See

It's a state of emergency for Black America. Most Black businesses are merely surviving rather than thriving, and the unemployment rate is at an all-time high. According to Dr. Claud Anderson, author of **PowerNomics: The National Plan to Empower Black America,** the hidden national unemployment rate of Blacks is 35%. In cities like Baltimore, Detroit, and Pittsburg, Black unemployment is well over 45%. In New York, unemployment for Black men tops 51%, and the national youth unemployment figure for Blacks is nearly 80%.

WALLACE DAVIS, A LOS ANGELES-BASED retired teacher, made the following statement
in his new book, *MOURNING: The Plight of Poor
Blacks and Poor Whites in America.* "This is the first
time in history where a generation of Blacks is worse
off than their parents."

Something is biblically and spiritually wrong with
this picture. Proverbs 13:22 states: A good man lea-
veth an inheritance to his children's children. Back
in the day, Black parents made every possible sacrifice to ensure a good education for their children.
Parents constantly reminded their children that they
had to be three times better than Whites in order to
compete in any race with Whites. My generation had
more education than our parents, and we understood
the sacrifice made by our parents. Therefore, it was
always in our conscious to provide for our parents in
their "golden age." Placing our parents in a home was
never an option for us.

Also during those days, when you mentioned the
word *minorities*, it was understood that the word ref-
erenced Blacks folks. However, today, this is not the
case. Now, the use of the word *minorities* is ambigu-
ous and broad and should not be used when calculat-
ing the needs and conditions of Black America.

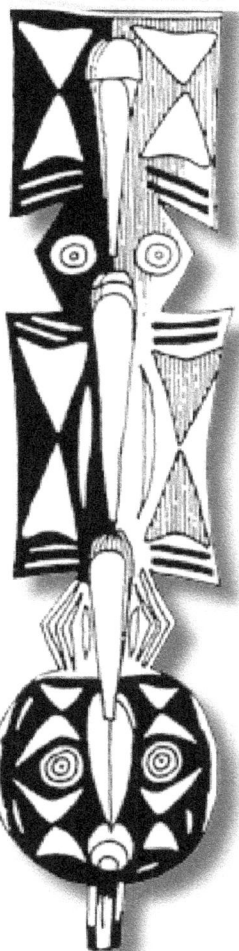

What Happened?

WE CEASED TO VALUE FAMILY. We became self-centered and greedy. We wanted to imitate our oppressor in all his ways. We strayed from our African cultural. We ceased being our brother's keeper. We became obsessed with instant gratification—no more layaways for us—right now, baby. In our attempt to keep up with the Joneses, we spent our children's inheritance; we went for the "bling bling," too. We purchased five-bedroom homes when we only needed two or three bedrooms. No more sharing. We had to have a bedroom for each child and each had to have his/her own television in their room, and we had to have a television in the living room, den, and kitchen. We

stopped eating together. Now, everybody eats when they are ready. We stopped blessing the food, which is a symbol of gratitude. We stopped saying our prayers before going to bed. We stopped demanding that our children go to church and started asking them if they were going to go to church.

What Has It Cost us?

WHAT HAS IT COST US? Our children are less educated than their parents, and many do not see the value of a college education because of the conditions they witness in many Blacks who are educated—including their parents. Parents are financially providing for their unemployed grown children who live in their home, and in far too many cases, are providing for their grandchildren because their grandchildren's parents are unemployed or on drugs or are incarcerated. This is a guarantee for the perpetuation of poverty.

Where Else Did We Go Wrong?

WHERE ELSE DID WE GO WRONG? It happened when we shifted away from vocational training/the trades, and focused on college education only. This was a big mistake! Vocation trades could lead to self-reliance and self-determination. We placed more emphasis on professional careers than vocational careers. We abandoned our Black-owned businesses for the sake of integration—this was the origin of our economic demise.

We must find ways to correct the wrongs, and it's going to take a concerted effort from all of us. The church, which used to be the pillar of the Black community, must return to its role. By any means necessary, we must restore and

revive the economic status of Black America. If we fail to do this within the next five years, then this generation and the generations to come will become permanent, modern-day slaves. Our forefathers fought hard to end slavery for themselves and for their offspring. Their blood is buried deep in America's soil. Their bones lay at the bottom of the Mississippi River. How dare we lock up in our gated communities while our offspring are being placed in predicaments that will land them in the "new slave ship," packed in like sardines, a ship that does not sail—better known as—PRISON. Economic and financial literacy is everybody's business.

What Must We Do?

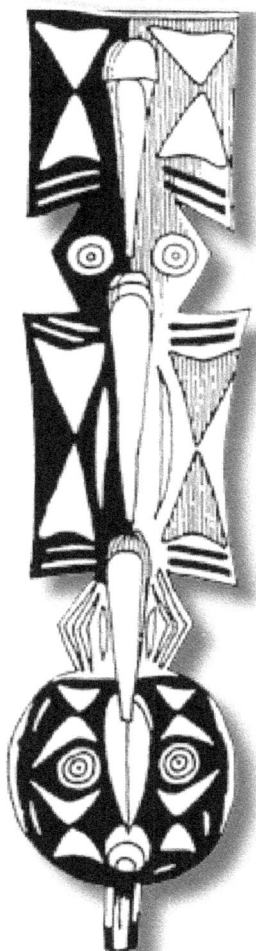

WE MUST TAKE RADICAL AND unpopular action. We must understand that we must pack our own parachute. It's like this: We are all on the airplane called America. This plane is losing oxygen, and we must remove the mask and place it over our face first. Blacks must save themselves first. Other races are already living by these principles. I am not angry at them; I am angry and disappointed with Black America for being STUPID!

And I will not apologize for saying STUPID.

If a mother allows everyone to nurse from her breast and will not feed her own

baby, that's STUPID. It goes beyond ignorant because you know better—so it's plain, ole STUPID.

LET'S LOOK AT A FEW EXAMPLES OF STUPIDITY

1. We continue to believe that a college degree is the answer to our economic crisis. Dr. Claud Anderson writes an article called "Will Black Scholars Have Jobs?" in The Harvest Institute Newsletter. Hear his words: "Black parents admonish their children to get a good education and work hard and success will follow. But the direct connection between education and employment has weakened according to a March 22, 2006, Washington Post column titled, "Will Your Job Survive?" (A21) Columnist Harold Meyerson warns in this article of the serious threat that globalization poses to the near-term future of the U.S. In 1994, economist Jeremy Rifkin, in his book, The End of Work, issued a similar warning. He said that only 25% of the jobs that existed then would exist in the workplace by the year 2015. Having said this and knowing that Blacks are the last hired and the first to be laid off or fired, the future for Black

employment and economic improvement appears bleak.

2. Only 25% of college graduates are working in the field of their study. And in years past, 75% of Black college graduates worked for the government. This is not today's reality—now Whites and immigrants dominate the government jobs. Do most of these government workers have a college degree? The answer is, no! Other factors to consider: The out-of-country outsourcing, and the in-house prison outsourcing, which provides free or cheap labor, adds to the bleak outlook for Black America. If Blacks follow this path and believe that things will change without their personal involvement in making things happen for them, that's STUPID!

3. If you think our educational system has the intent to educate Black children to be able to compete and to displace Whites and other races, you are STUPID. Blacks need to educate their children. Would a rat send his little mice to a cat school? Today in our inner-city schools, Black teachers are a disappearing act. But Black parents do not seem to be concerned about who

teaches their babies. What do you think White parents would think, feel, and do, if their children attended a school where 95% of the teachers were Black?

4. Blacks continue to complain about the maltreatment and disrespect towards them while doing business with non-Black business owners, yet these businesses continue to flourish in the community. When Blacks have a problem with a Black-owned business, (1) they fail to report it to the owner of the business. (2) They make up their minds to never patronize that business again, nor any other Black business that provides that same service. (3) They spread the word about that Black business in hopes that the business will be forced to close its doors. Blacks have a silent code of conduct by which Black-owned businesses must abide. They do not hold non-Black businesses to the same standards of service. When a Black person is treated wrongly by a White business or other non-black business, they never say, "I will never do business again with a White business or Asian business, etc. etc." This is the epitome of STUPID!

5. Black people help to build Black churches with their hard-earned money, their Social Security money, and their welfare money (people on welfare pay tithes, too) for a building that remains locked up most of the week. There is enough food in the food banks to feed most of the hungry and homeless people in the Black community and the churches have access to the food banks, yet they will not open their doors to feed the people. There are many unemployed and retired people in the church who could distribute the food to the poor, but they don't. What's wrong here?

BLACKS HAVE THE attitude that "I am not going to concern myself with what the church or pastor does with the money when I give my tithes. I leave it up to God to handle everything." That sounds good, but that's STUPID. We must all be held accountable to man and to God.

6. Politically, we are so incorrect in how we play politics. We continue to vote without asking for any benefits. Once the Black politician is in office, you will hear a conversation like this: "We must hold our politicians accountable." I must ask, though,

accountable to what? What did he promise you? We continue to allow corrupt Black politicians to mark the election ballots for us, and we ask no questions about their past performance. Now that's STUPID.

7. Too many Black professionals do not come back nor give back to the Black community. They don't come back to spend money with Black-owned businesses in the community. They do not give to the causes that help empower the Black community. They become Beverly Hills and Hollywood shoppers. Many of them who are in business, locate their businesses outside of the Black community, even when a majority of their clients are Black.

Here's What We Must Do!

I will give you some of my thoughts, being a business owner in the community for more than 30-years-plus.

1. Read *PowerNomics: The National Plan to Empower Black America*. We do not need to reinvent the wheel. Dr. Anderson, the author of *PowerNomics*, has laid out a master plan for every facet of life. In chapter five, Economic Action Plan #6, the heading reads: Construct vertical businesses and industries that control all processes from raw resources in markets within and out-

side of Black communities. Dr. Anderson states, "We will have our greatest impact if we exercise vertical involvement primarily within those businesses in which we have some competitive advantages. We should seek out key industries and strive to create a monopoly."

2. We must make vocational trades and business ownership an option for our children when choosing a career. You must demand that your child learn conversational Spanish and Chinese. We must determine the curriculum for the schools in our community, which are based on the global and local trend. Demand courses in Home Economics, Financial Literacy, Parenting, and Conflict Resolution.

3. Encourage your children to become educators. There is a need, and there is a demand. Remember, if you choose a double major, let teaching be one of them. If all else fails, you can always teach and be able to provide a decent living for you and your family if you are financially savvy. A predominately Black school should have at least 50% Black teachers.

4. For the next two years, all students who are not doing well in reading, writing, and ba-

sic math should be pulled from traditional schooling. Churches should open their doors for a non-traditional school setting, utilizing retired teachers and housewives who have basic skills proficiency. Teach only reading, writing, and basic math. Do not be tricked. One does not need a degree to teach our kids basic skills. Our forefathers were taught these skills by teachers who had only completed high school, and some of their teachers did not even complete high school. Let's take control of our children's education. Our schools have failed our children, so now it's up to us.

A student who has not mastered basic skills like reading, writing, and math is being set up for failure for all other classes, make no mistake about it. The ability to master basic skills, and not just barely passing these classes is a must. The student's ability to be successfully in all other classes is dependent upon their ability to read with comprehension, so do not allow the school system to program your child for failure.

In order to change things, we must get RADICALLY RADICAL! If a school does not have books available for students and will not offer a curriculum that's necessary

for the success of your children, all parents should boycott such schools until positive changes are made in the school. That's radical. Don't be scared to fight for your children. One thing's for sure—if we keep on doing what we have been doing, our children will keep on getting what they have been getting. Is that what you want?

5. Develop a code of conduct by which all businesses in the community must adhere to. Develop a Council of Elders to oversee problems and conflicts in the business community. Any business where its conduct is out of line must be taken before the Council of Elders for sanction. If corrections are not made, the entire community must boycott that business. And any member of the Black community who continues to patronize that business must be dealt with.

6. Go out of your way to shop with a Black business. Make that a priority. Remember, your children will do what they see you do and our economic future is dependent upon this behavior. When displeased with the service of a Black business, let the owner know and give the business another chance. Do not bad-mouth the business,

because after all, the problem could have been caused by you. Customers are not always right in real life.

7. Start holding banquets and meetings away from hotels. Start utilizing church banquet halls and Masonic Lodge halls in the community. It does not cost much to decorate these places and make them real nice for your events. By doing this, you have just opened up much business for the Black catering services and many jobs for Black waiters will have been created. That's what I am talking about—economics. Other services besides catering can be developed along these same lines, like sewing factories for our clothing.

8. Churches should get food from food banks and feed those in need. Pastors should open church doors and make their facilities available for community use. Open up non-traditional schools for children in the community in churches during the week.

Churches should share their sanctuaries with other ministries instead of these different ministries holding services in hotels or renting little hole in the wall, run-down buildings and trying to fix up property that

belongs to someone else. After all, churches should belong to the community. They are not private, for-profit organizations.

9. Professionals should come back to the community and start businesses as well as to support Black-owned businesses. Lawyers and doctors should give one day a month free service to the community. Teachers should give one day to tutor students who are struggling and falling behind in reading, writing, and math.

10. Superstars and celebrities should visit Black-owned businesses every six months to help bring attention to them. As you know, the media will follow the superstars and celebrities as they promote Black businesses.

Conclusion

We have many wrongs to make right, but we do not have a long time in which to do so. So let's get busy. Our economic future is dependent upon what we do today. Time is of the essence. We must pay close attention to the economic clock and the economic calendar on the wall because they serve as an almanac.

If mainstream America can conduct business globally with China, Japan, etc., why can't Blacks do the same? At the very least, we can conduct business on a domestic level. It's no reason for us Blacks not doing business with Black-owned businesses in Tennessee,

Georgia, etc. It's time that we think "outside the box." Our survival depends on such.

I have launched a Web site, www.911forblackamerica. com. The purpose of this site is to serve as a vehicle that connects Blacks globally. This Web site provides the following information: Domestic/Global business listings, Black-owned radio stations with a format that discusses Black issues., Black Internet radio talk shows that discuss Black issues, education and vocations that Blacks must seek for survival, current events that all Blacks should know about and MUCH MORE!

Let's do the right thing! And remember, all we have is each other—so let us stand together and let's force Blacks in every capacity to be responsible and accountable to us as a people.

I have included a report that was derived from the State of Black Los Angeles conducted by the United Way of Greater Los Angeles and the Los Angeles Urban League. It is a 41 page document. Certain critical indexes have been extracted from the study and have been positioned in such a way that one can view the ethnicity comparison at a glance.

The bleak picture of African Americans that you will see in the report is not to discourage Blacks, but rather to provide Blacks with information that I hope will motivate and encourage them to make swift and radical changes in their attitude and behavior towards business ownership and vocational training.

As you study the indexes, consider the role that you can play in helping to make a positive change. Even though this report is about the City of Los Angeles and the State of California, you will find similar disparities between Blacks and other races across the country—and the world at large.

As you observe the indexes such as business ownership, median household income, and the unemployment rate, you will clearly see the direct correlation between each of them.

I trust that this information will be the catalyst that will begin a dialogue among Blacks that will compel every Black family to pursue a path that will lead to self-determination for their family—and then for the community.

This report was merged by Dr. Rosie Milligan (excerpts from The State of Black Los Angeles and The State of Black California)

CALIFORNIA POPULATION BY RACE AND ETHINICITY 1990 &2000

1990 California		2000 California	
Whites	17,209,126	Whites	15,816,790
Blacks	2,092,446	Blacks	2,181,926
Latinos	3,805,349	Latinos	10,966,556
Asians	2,710,353	Asians	3,752,596
Others	240,158	Others	250,665

1990 Los Angeles		2000 Los Angeles	
Whites	3,618,850	Whites	2,959,614
Blacks	934,776	Blacks	901,472
Latino	3,351,242	Latino	4,242,213
Asians	907,810	Asians	1,147,834
Others	50,446	Others	45,544

Cities In California With The Largest Concentrations Of Blacks & Latino					
Blacks			Latino		
Los Angeles	901,472	9.7%	Los Angeles	4,242,213	45.6%
Oakland	297,975	12.9%	Oakland	441,686	19.2%
Inland Empire	242,604	7.6%	Inland Empire	1,228,962	38.7%
San Diego	154,487	5.7%	San Diego	750,965	27.5%

Percentage of California Populations by Race and Ethnicity 2000	
Whites	48.0%
Blacks	6.6%
Latino	33.3%
Asians	11.4%
Others	0.8%

The largest concentrations of Blacks are found in Oakland at about 13 percent followed by Sacramento with 10.1% and Los Angeles with 9.7%

MEDIAN HOUSEHOLD
INCOME ECONOMIC INDEX

California		Los Angeles	
Whites	53,734	Whites	53,978
Blacks	34,956	Blacks	31,905
Latinos	36,532	Latinos	33,820
Asians	55,366	Asians	47,631

Business Ownership			
California		Los Angeles	
Whites	1,827,734	Whites	489,284
Blacks	79,110	Blacks	38,277
Latinos	336,405	Latinos	136,678
Asians	316,048	Asians	114,462

Unemployment Rate			
California		Los Angeles	
Whites	5.0%	Whites	5.8%
Blacks	12.0%	Blacks	13.8%
Latinos	10.1%	Latinos	9.9%
Asians	5.2%	Asians	5.8%

Poverty Rate			
California		Los Angeles	
Whites	7.8%	Whites	8.5%
Blacks	22.4%	Blacks	24.4%
Latinos	22.1%	Latinos	24.2%
Asians	12.8%	Asians	13.9%

HEALTH INDEX

State of California		Los Angeles	
Life Expectancy		**Life Expectancy**	
Whites	77.3	Whites	77.3
Blacks	71.1	Blacks	71.1
Latinos	82.5	Latinos	82.5
Asians	83.7	Asians	83.7
Adolescent Mortality Rate		**Adolescent Mortality Rate**	
Whites	44.0	Whites	61.7
Blacks	81.2	Blacks	131.4
Latinos	46.4	Latinos	77.9
Asians	38.02	Asians	58.2
Homicide Rate Males		**Homicide Rate Males**	
Whites	4.54	Whites	6.6
Blacks	41.03	Blacks	78.0
Latinos	13.69	Latinos	18.7
Asians	5.11	Asians	5.5
Homicide Rate Females		**Homicide Rate Females**	
Whites	2.13	Whites	2.3
Blacks	7.14	Blacks	7.9
Latinos	2.21	Latinos	2.9
Asians	2.58	Asians	2.2
Homicide Rate Adolescent		**Homicide Rate Adolescent**	
Whites	1.6	Whites	0.1
Blacks	8.4	Blacks	11.4
Latinos	3.5	Latinos	4.1
Asians	3.4	Asians	1.8
Infant Death Rate (per 1000 live birth)		**Infant Death Rate (per 1000 live birth)**	
Whites	4.8	Whites	5.0
Blacks	11.6	Blacks	13.0
Latinos	5.2	Latinos	5.0
Asians	4.1	Asians	4.0
Death Rate All Causes (per 100,000)		**Death Rate All Causes (per 100,000)**	
Whites	846.0	Whites	700.0
Blacks	1,139.5	Blacks	979.0
Latinos	634.5	Latinos	540.0
Asians	532.6	Asians	445.0

9 7 8 0 9 8 1 5 7 8 3 0 9